2012

THE LIFE CYCLE OF A

Salmon

By Colleen Sexton

BLASTOFF!
READERS
3

BELLWETHER MEDIA • MINNEAPOLIS, MN

Note to Librarians, Teachers, and Parents:

Blastoff! Readers are carefully developed by literacy experts and combine standards-based content with developmentally appropriate text.

Level 1 provides the most support through repetition of high-frequency words, light text, predictable sentence patterns, and strong visual support.

Level 2 offers early readers a bit more challenge through varied simple sentences, increased text load, and less repetition of high-frequency words.

Level 3 advances early-fluent readers toward fluency through increased text and concept load, less reliance on visuals, longer sentences, and more literary language.

Level 4 builds reading stamina by providing more text per page, increased use of punctuation, greater variation in sentence patterns, and increasingly challenging vocabulary.

Level 5 encourages children to move from "learning to read" to "reading to learn" by providing even more text, varied writing styles, and less familiar topics.

Whichever book is right for your reader, Blastoff! Readers are the perfect books to build confidence and encourage a love of reading that will last a lifetime!

This edition first published in 2010 by Bellwether Media, Inc.

No part of this publication may be reproduced in whole or in part without written permission of the publisher. For information regarding permission, write to Bellwether Media, Inc., Attention: Permissions Department, 5357 Penn Avenue South Minneapolis, MN 55419.

Library of Congress Cataloging-in-Publication Data
Sexton, Colleen A., 1967-
  The life cycle of a salmon / by Colleen Sexton.
    p. cm. – (Blastoff! Readers life cycles)
  Includes bibliographical references and index.
  Summary: "Developed by literacy experts for students in kindergarten through grade three, this book follows salmon as they transform from eggs to adults. Through leveled text and related images, young readers will watch these creatures grow through every stage of life"–Provided by publisher.
  ISBN 978-1-60014-311-3 (hardcover : alk. paper)
  1. Salmon–Life cycles–Juvenile literature. I. Title.
  QL638.S2S43 2010
  597.5'6–dc22
                              2009037343

Text copyright © 2010 by Bellwether Media, Inc. BLASTOFF! READERS and associated logos are trademarks and/or registered trademarks of Bellwether Media, Inc.

Printed in the United States of America, North Mankato, MN.
010110   1149

Contents

Salmon are fish with shiny scales.
They are powerful swimmers.

Most fish live in either saltwater or freshwater. Salmon can live in both. They swim in oceans, lakes, rivers, and streams.

Salmon grow in stages. The stages of a salmon's **life cycle** are egg, **alevin**, **fry**, **smolt**, and adult.

egg

alevin

fry

smolt

adult

Salmon begin life as eggs in a shallow stream. The baby salmon that grow inside the eggs are called alevins.

The alevins hatch in three to four months. They wiggle out of their eggs and into the water. They cannot swim yet.

The alevins do not eat. They live off the **yolks** of their eggs. The alevins carry the yolks in sacs under their bodies.

The alevins grow teeth
and fins. Their scales
get darker. Their yolk
sacs disappear.

The alevins are now fry. The fry swim and learn to hunt young **insects** for food.

The fry eat and grow for about a year. They begin to look like adult salmon. They have become smolts.

The smolts make a long journey. They follow the **currents** of streams and rivers all the way to the ocean.

The smolts stay in areas where freshwater rivers meet the saltwater ocean. Their bodies must get used to saltwater before they swim out to sea.

The smolts are now adult salmon. They hunt **krill** and small fish. They keep growing.

Adult salmon get ready to **spawn** a few years later. They find the river that brought them to the ocean.

The salmon swim up the river. They fight the strong current. They jump over rocks and logs. They even climb up waterfalls!

At last the salmon reach the place where they hatched.

The females use their tails to dig nests called **redds**. Males wait nearby.

Females lay eggs in the redds. Then the males **fertilize** the eggs.

The salmon are worn out after their long journey. Most adults die after spawning. Their eggs are the start of a new life cycle!

Glossary

alevin—a newly hatched salmon that has an egg sac attached to it

current—the movement of water in rivers, streams, and oceans

fertilize—when an egg from a female joins with special cells called sperm from a male; an alevin will grow only in an egg that has been fertilized.

fry—a young salmon that has used up its yolk and can feed itself

insect—a small animal with six legs and a body divided into three parts; salmon eat the young form of insects that live in water.

krill—tiny sea animals that look like shrimp; krill are the main food of salmon.

life cycle—the stages of life of an animal; a life cycle includes being born, growing up, having young, and dying.

redd—a fish's nest; female salmon dig several redds at the bottom of a shallow stream when they spawn.

smolt—a young salmon that is large enough to make the journey to the ocean

spawn—a way of breeding in which the female lays eggs and then the male fertilizes them

yolk—part of an egg that is food for an animal

To Learn More

AT THE LIBRARY
Kalman, Bobbie. *The Life Cycle of a Salmon*. New York, N.Y.: Crabtree Publishing, 2007.

LeBox, Annette. *Salmon Creek*. Toronto, Ont.: Douglas & McIntyre, 2002.

Suzuki, David. *Salmon Forest*. New York, N.Y.: GreyStone Books, 2003.

ON THE WEB
Learning more about life cycles is as easy as 1, 2, 3.

1. Go to www.factsurfer.com.

2. Enter "life cycles" into the search box.

3. Click the "Surf" button and you will see a list of related Web sites.

With factsurfer.com, finding more information is just a click away.

Index

The images in this book are reproduced through the courtesy of: Jeff Foott, front cover (egg), pp. 7, 8, 18-19; Bruce Coleman Inc. / Alamy, front cover (alevin), pp. 6 (alevin); 9; Alaska Stock Images, front cover (fry), pp. 6 (fry), 11; ImageState, front cover (adult), p. 16; Renee Demartin/Kimballstock, pp. 4-5; age fotostock, p. 6 (egg); The Image Bank, pp. 6 (smolt), 12-13; Tom & Pat Leeson/Kimballstock, p. 6 (adult); Lucidio Studio, Inc. / Alamy, p. 10; Sergey Gorshkov, p. 14; Paul Nicklen, p. 15; Gary Vestal, p. 17; Natural Visions / Alamy, p. 20; All Canada Photos, p. 21.